The Power ot

"NO!"
for Women

When to Say It. How to Say It.
And What to Do When You Hear It.

CRYSTEL LYNN SMITH

Willow Keep Publishing
P.O. Box 54, Front Royal, VA

For information:
Crystel Clear Business Strategies
P.O. Box 104 Gore Virginia 22637

ISBN: 9781088502037

INTRODUCTION

There just aren't enough hours in the day!
I need another me! I need to learn to say no!

Women are amazing creatures. We are caregivers for our elderly, breadwinners for our families, team players for our employers, volunteers in our communities. We are prayer warriors in our church, leaders of our PTOs, reliable members of our groups, nurturers of our children, and supporters of our significant others. We are cheerleaders of our friends, drivers of the extracurricular, chef of our kitchens, organizers of chaos, and schedulers of all that must be done.

We are givers of our time, our finances, our love, our material possessions and ourselves. We will empty our cup that has not been filled for months on end and yet wonder why we feel overwhelmed and downright exhausted.

We will give the brand new or wrinkled shirt right off our back if it doesn't leave us naked in public. And even then, we heavily consider giving our shirts before we decide that naked in public may not be the wisest decision we could make.

We over-promise, never wanting to let anyone down. We feel overwhelmed, under accomplished, even overcome with guilt at times, and wonder why we just can't utter that dirty little word – no.

The Power of "No!" for Women will provide you, my amazing woman friend, the opportunity to have a pivotal and profound moment in your life, just as I did seven years ago, and to finally begin to feel accomplished, productive, successful and able to live a life that you are excited to wake up to every day – possibly after having a great night's rest.

Imagine that!

CONTENTS

1

MY PLEASURE

Need a ride to work? I'm your girl! Someone to talk to? Call me! Want some help around the house? Certainly! Take the kids to their sporting events? I'm headed that way anyway! Dinner? Of course! Laundry washed, dried, folded and hung? I've got this! Work late? You betcha! Team mom? All over it! Meet for lunch? I'll be there! Buy you a cup of coffee? It would be my pleasuuurrrre! Sound familiar?

I left the coffee shop overwhelmed, almost crippled, with anxiety and guilt. By the time I walked across the street to my car I was in tears. In my car, I immediately began to question and beat myself up.

You really said yes? Why didn't you JUST SAY NO? How are you going to explain this to your family? What are your grandchildren going to think? How are you going to make this up to them?

How could you have done this to your family? You need to learn to say NO, Crystel!

This conversation with myself lasted the entire 45-minute ride home, continued to wake me up nightly, and haunted me for years to come.

2

WHAT TIME SUNDAY?

During one of our coaching sessions John and I discovered that if we could increase the average dollar sale by only $5.00, his coffee shop would profit an additional $300,000.00 a year. I can remember the excitement when we ran the projections!

Do you know what $300,000.00 can do for a small business owner? John could hire the additional staff they desperately needed. They would have greater buying power, reduce the cost of their products, and increase profit margins. John could take a salary and possibly even a vacation or two! This was a huge breakthrough! There was only one problem. His team had never been encouraged to offer their customers anything other than the traditional cup of coffee and John certainly didn't want his team to feel like they were there to just sell products.

This coffee shop was more than just a place where the customers came to buy coffee. It was the heart of downtown, where families gathered on a winter's day, with cups of hot chocolate warming their hands, sharing laughter and sometimes sadness, while Miss Martha served them just as she did her own family. It was where professionals met, grabbed a cup of coffee and got to work. It wasn't a pushy sales place as John said.

While John was hesitant to encourage his team to offer their customers more, he was excited about the opportunity that upselling would bring to him, his business, employees, and customers. John and I finally came to an agreement. We would train his team to offer their customers everything <u>they</u> thought their customers would enjoy.

John was a strong businessman. However, upselling and training his team to upsell were not his strengths. You guessed it and John knew it. Selling and training were my strengths. After all, if I was the expert wasn't I the obvious choice to train John's team? I was excited about the opportunity to teach the team how to serve their customers breakfast rather than just a cup of coffee. I knew that the business would grow. John's employees could be paid more, and he could finally be paid for his hard work. Their customers would enjoy delicious food and spend more time with their families over breakfast. This is the stuff that drives me!

Then, he asked the question, "Would you be available to provide a training on a Sunday? It's the only day we are closed early, and I can get everyone here."

My internal struggle and conversation began. *John needs me. If I don't give them this training, he may never get to take a vacation. Miss Martha may never earn the money she truly needs to support her family. John may even be upset with me. No, Sundays are my church and family days. After church, my children, grandchildren, parents and I all gather in my home. We spend the entire day catching up, playing board games, cheering on our favorite football team, eating way too much food, and making the most precious memories. No, Crystel. You cannot provide a training on a Sunday. Just say it! He will understand. There will be another day. Just say no!*

After a few moments of silence, I was finally able to squeak out, "Sure, what time Sunday works for you?"

3

DRIVING IN SLOW MOTION

5-year-old Mason and 3-year-old Addy came running, yelling, *"Grandmaaaaa!"* and jumped into my arms as they did every Sunday. Even though we spent every Sunday together, there was always new excitement to be together. Our home was once again filled with family, the smell of chili warming in the crockpot, countertops buried under the best football snacks, every inch of the living room taken with family, board games, and puzzles. It was perfect – <u>until</u> I made the announcement.

I shared with my family that I had to leave to provide a training for one of my clients. I'll never forget the look on my children's and grandchildren's faces as they looked up at me from the floor, where they were playing Monopoly, with such disbelief and disappointment.

"What? You're leaving? But why grandma? It's Sunday. It's our family day."

I felt as if my heart was literally breaking. I lump began to well up in my throat and it was all I could do to hold back the tears. I explained again that I had to go to work. I apologized profusely and said I would only be working this one Sunday.

"I still don't understand. We always have family time on Sundays. Why would you go to work when we're here?"

I didn't have a good answer. I didn't have any answer. I was asking myself the same question. *Why would I leave my family, my precious grandchildren on the one day that we all cherished each week?*

I apologized again, gathered my things, I kissed and hugged Mason and Addy, told them I'd be back soon, and walked out the door.

It was the longest 45-minute drive of my life. I couldn't get there fast enough. It was as if I was driving in slow motion. I saw their sad little faces over and over. I must have replayed that hour 10 times in my mind by the time I arrived at the coffee shop. It was time to get myself together, focus, and deliver what I had promised, exceptional training for my client.

The team was reserved at first. I expected as much. They had never been trained to sell. They had only been trained to serve. If I'm going to be completely honest with you. I allowed myself to feel frustrated. How could they be almost dismissive in the first few minutes of our meeting? Didn't they realize what I had given up so I could be there to serve them? Didn't they see that I could have been home with my family, my most precious gifts, on a Sunday evening? Instead, I drove 45 minutes, was going to spend two hours working with them, and then another 45 minutes driving home?

I made a choice at that moment to choose a new perspective. Because it was my choice to be there. I was the one who agreed to provide the training. I was the one who said yes. It was my responsibility to provide a training that would give them these incredible opportunities. I was grateful to have John as a client and honored that he chose and trusted me to share my knowledge with his team.

Within the next 5 minutes we were laughing, they were engaged and learning! John and his team thanked me for spending my Sunday evening with them and for providing an educational and fun training session. They were excited to begin to offer their clients breakfast, make more money, and see their customers enjoying meals together! The evening was a success and my heart was full! Until the drive home.

4

THE SIMULTANEOUS NO

I drove as fast as I legally could. I had to get back to my family and try to salvage what was left of the evening. Again, I replayed leaving my family in my head, asking myself over and over the question Mason had asked. Why would I leave my home when my family was there? Why didn't I just say no? In that very moment, it hit me like a ton, no, 100 ton, of bricks! I had, in fact, said no!

The very moment I said yes to John I simultaneously said no to spending the day with my grandchildren. I said no to the sweetest cuddles, to losing game after game to a five and three-year-old, to reminiscing with my father, my son and my daughter. I said no to laughing with my step-mother, to sharing delicious food, to cheering on our football team. I said no cherishing my family and making precious memories! This was a pivotal, profound, painful, and life-changing moment for me! My hope is that what follows will be profound and life-changing for you as well.

The truth is you say no countless times every day and don't even realize it. <u>Every time you say yes to something, you are simultaneously saying no to something else.</u>

When I said yes to John. I simultaneously said no to spending the day with my family. We say yes to people, actions, responsibilities and at the same time say no to ourselves, other people, actions or responsibilities.

If you've said yes to working late, wishing you would have had the strength to say no, you did, in fact, say no. You may have said no to spending time with your family. Maybe you said no to getting the rest you desperately need or reading that book you've promised yourself you'd get to for the last month. Whatever the yes, there is always the simultaneous no!

How many times have you said to yourself, friends, family, coworkers *"I need to learn to say no!"* The harsh truth is you don't need to *learn to say no*. You're the expert and the master of saying no. It comes so naturally to you, you do it without even realizing that you're saying it – or what and who you're saying it to!

Since that day I've never worked another Sunday. I've never said no to my family days. As a matter of fact, I've never said I need to learn to say no again. And you don't have to either!

It will take some practice in the beginning. However, if you will practice this, I promise you will never again find yourself having the same conversations with yourself, beating yourself up about your lack of ability to say no.

The first thing you must do is share this concept with everyone in your life! The next is this. EVERY TIME someone asks you to do something, you must tell them that in order to say yes you must first understand what or who you are saying no to. If you're comfortable with what you have to say no to, in order to do what they've asked, the answer is yes. If not, then share what you will have to say no to and ask them to understand that it is not something or someone you are willing to say no to.

If a friend asks you to join a board that meets every Friday evening you may find it hard to say no. After all, she's been such a good friend. She would do it if you asked her to. And the non-profit provides amazing support in your community. How could you say no? Here's how. You explain to your friend that by saying yes to spending Friday

13

evenings at the board meeting you would be saying no spending time with your family (or whatever you would have to say no to).

Recently, I've shared with my friends that saying yes to dinner with them meant that I would have to say no finishing my book. Which ultimately meant no to sharing this life-changing message with thousands of women.

We even say no to our own success without realizing it. By saying yes to sleeping in (which is what you're doing) you may be saying no to getting to the gym. By saying yes to watching your favorite television show you may be saying no to getting the rest you need. By saying yes to all of your friends' requests you may be saying no eating healthy, pursuing your passion, or personal growth.

We sabotage our own financial success. Not by saying no, but by saying yes to frivolous spending. We simultaneously said no to saving or investing money.

As women, we say no to ourselves far more often than we say no to anyone or anything else.

We feel the need to serve everyone and everything. We are the ones who stay late at work, possibly saying no to spending time with our families. We are the ones who then feel guilty about working late and then stay up late to clean the house, do the laundry, and make sure the children have lunches packed for school, saying no to the rest we need. We are board members, team moms, PTO leaders, pet sitters, babysitters, volunteers, church members, wives, nurturing mothers, loving sisters, amazing aunts, fun grandmothers – every single day! And we wonder why we become overwhelmed with our daily lives. I'll tell you why. It's not because we need to learn to say no. It's because we do say no to ourselves, over, and over again.

From today forward your internal conversations will not be filled with frustration and guilt about not saying no. They will sound like this. *If I say yes to _____ that means I am saying no _____.* If you're okay with what you must say no to then yes, it is. If you're not, then the answer is no.

In every internal and external conversation, you must consciously choose.

If you are changing your eating habits to become healthy and have a craving for an unhealthy snack, your conversation may sound like this: If I say yes to this ice cream I'm

saying no to being healthy, breathing better, walking far-
ther, wearing a size _____.

If you are saying yes to taking a nap it may sound like this.
*If I say yes to an hour of sleep, I am saying no to getting that closet
organized, being more efficient and happier in the mornings.*

If a friend asks you to volunteer for an event your conversation may sound like this. *If I say yes to volunteering this
Saturday, I would have to say no to spending time with my husband.
You can understand why I am choosing to spend time with my husband right?*

Sometimes what you must say no to is okay. If someone
asks you to have a business lunch meeting you may decide
you have to say no to mopping the floors which you're not
a fan of anyway. In that case, lunch it is!

My daughter asked me to go to the gym with her. It was
10:30 at night. I was exhausted, to say the least. I wanted
to stay in bed and sleep. I began the process. If I say yes
to an extra hour of sleep. I am simultaneously saying no
to spending time with my daughter, laughing, increasing
my strength, reducing my weight, feeling better, and making memories with her. I chose to say no to that extra hour
of sleep. To the gym, we went!

The key to saying no with compassion, fairness, without guilt and consistency is twofold. One, recognize that _every_ yes is a simultaneous no. Two, create the habit of making a conscious choice internally and externally of what or who you are saying no to.

5

THE RATIONAL LIE

We rationalize or try to make peace with what we've said yes, or no to. It will just take a couple of hours. It's only a couple of dollars. She would do it for me. I can start my diet tomorrow. I can get it done next weekend. I can sleep in on Saturday.

Let's face it. It may only be a couple of dollars. And by saying yes to loaning your friend money you may be saying no to having enough money for something you truly need. It may only be a couple of hours. And you may be saying no to reading a bedtime story to your child. She just might have done it for you. And you may be saying no to the rest you need. It may be a great new pair of shoes. And you may be saying no to investing in your financial future.

At some point in my internal conversation, I rationalized saying yes to training and no to my family on that Sunday.

19

It's only one Sunday. They will still have fun without me. I can make it up to them next Sunday. They need some bonding time without me there anyway. I got to spend a couple of hours with them before I had to leave. I had a long list of rationale. Which, by the way, isn't rational at all. It's merely lying to yourself to alleviate the pain, frustration, and possible guilt you feel when you give your simultaneous no.

Rationalizing or making peace with your yes (simultaneous no) is a dangerous place to live. It will always lead to the next reason, the next lie, the next internal conversation, the next frustration, and the next simultaneous no.

This proverbial hamster wheel of yesses can be disastrous to you, your family, your health, and ultimately your life. By saying yes to staying on the hamster wheel are you saying no to family memories, a healthy marriage, your physical and mental health, your relationship with God, personal growth, financial success? Which is it?

If you are the yes woman (simultaneous no woman) eventually something will break. It may be your family, your marriage, your career, your health, your mental wellbeing, or your relationship with God.

We must stop telling ourselves these lies, stand firm in what we are saying yes to, and allow all of those who ask of our time, financial resources, and abilities, the opportunity to do the same.

If you find yourself rationalizing, making peace, lying to yourself it's time to pick up the phone and have the conversation you should have had to begin with.

Hi _____, I said yes to _____. While I would like to _____, I've realized that by saying yes to _____ I must say no to _____. I hope you understand that I have to say yes to _____ instead.

6

THE INTENTIONAL LIE

You've rationalized with lies to yourself and I bet you've lied to others to avoid saying the word no. *I would love to come to your Pampered Chef party. but I don't have a babysitter. Oh, my husband? He doesn't keep the children alone. Actually, he has to be in bed by 8:00. Yes, I could be home by 8:00. but the children take their baths at 7:00 and you know we have 3 children, so it takes both of us. I just hate that I'm going to have to miss it!*

As women, we reprimand our children for lying. We may dare our coworkers to lie to us about completing their tasks or their whereabouts. Heaven forbid our spouses lie to us about what they've done around the house. Yet, we are so fearful of the word no that we will without hesitation replace it with a 5-minute lie. and then feel guilty about lying <u>and</u> not attending the party!

I will never understand why it is easier for women to conjure up some cockamamy story about why they aren't able to do something than it is to merely say no. I will also say that I've been guilty of the same. *Crystel, can you come in and work from 8-6 on Saturday?*

Rather than politely saying no and explaining that if I said yes to working on Saturday, I'd have to say no to spending time with my family, I said I *would*, but I'd already promised to pick the grandchildren up and spend the day with them. Then I began to rationalize this lie. Double dangerous! I was going to spend the day with my grandchildren even if I hadn't promised to pick them up. Then the internal conversation began.

Why didn't you just tell him spending time with your family was more important? What if he finds out you really didn't promise the grandbabies that you would pick them up? You are such a hypocrite. You've always told your children that they can come to you with anything, to always tell the truth and it can be resolved. You've raised them to know that with lying comes consequences. And now you're the liar!

This was another pivotal moment for me. I realized that by choosing to lie, and it was a choice, <u>my choice</u>. My resistance to saying no caused me even greater grief. I had brought the frustration and grief upon myself. Never again have I lied to avoid saying no. I challenge you to free yourself of the guilt and grief of replacing no with a lie, even if it's an ever so slightly altered lie. The next time you are asked to join, volunteer, work, help with something, and are considering telling a lie, remember the only person who will have consequences to that lie is you. You can suffer the consequences, or you can reap the reward. The choice is yours. Choose wisely.

Since that moment I have said no to countless requests with great confidence and great reward. I spend more time with my family. I wake up excited to spend the day with those I've chosen to and doing the things that I place the highest value in accomplishing. My relationship with my family is incredibly blessed. I have a close relationship with the Lord. Close as in we chat all day every day. My business and my clients are thriving. I'm blessed to have some of the most remarkable clients who chose me to walk alongside this journey of business life with them. I'm able to continuously write and share the messages the Lord has put on my heart.

Today will be the day you begin to remove the lies, share the truth of your "no's", and live the life you are intended to live!

7

THE SUBLIMINAL LIE

As women, we say *I need to say to no* because we <u>*think*</u> we don't have enough time or resources to achieve the things in life we want to achieve or even to accomplish our daily tasks. It leaves us feeling frustrated, overwhelmed, unsuccessful and at times completely exhausted. And it's our own fault.

There aren't enough hours in the day. There just isn't enough time. These subliminal lies you tell yourself every day will eventually cost you your ability to reason, productivity, accomplishments, and success.

My friend Shanna recently posted a question to her Facebook followers. She asked her audience of women what they would do with an extra hour every day. The responses began to pour in. *Read, work on my business, spend time with my family, marketing, clean my house, write.*

I couldn't resist. I had to share some brutal truths with these women. My response was something like this. *I have to challenge each of you. If you had an extra hour every day, you would be doing the exact same things that you're doing right now, because time is not the challenge. It is what you choose to do with your time that leaves you feeling like you need more of it.*

While every one of those women shared what they <u>would do</u> if they had extra time in their day (read, spend time with family), they were socializing on social media <u>rather than doing</u> the thing <u>they said</u> they would do if they had more time.

Those women didn't need an extra hour. They needed to say yes to reading, to writing, spending time with their family and no to social media.

However, it's much easier to blame the lack of time or demands of the day than it is to take responsibility for and ownership of our choices.

The reality is we all have the same 24 hours each day. The only thing you can change is what *you* choose to do with *your* 24 hours – by choosing what you will say yes, and simultaneously say no to.

My business partner, Sherri, and I decided to provide a workshop to help business owners and their team members prioritize, become efficient, and effective with their time. We titled the workshop, <u>Time Management, the Truest Waste of Time. You Must Manage YOU!</u> Over the next several weeks the registration remained empty.

When we reached out to potential attendees the responses were full of subliminal lies. *I just don't have time. I need another me to get everything done I need to do. I would come if it were closer. I don't have time to spend in the car.*

I knew that they were lying to themselves and decided to prove it. I changed the workshop title from <u>Time Management the Truest Waste of Time. You must Manage You!</u> to <u>Time Management</u>.

Immediately the class began to fill! The challenge was never time. It was their choice to say no to taking responsibility and ownership of their time.

You cannot manage time. No matter how hard you may try, there is no physical way to stop, slow down, speed up, change, or manage time. The ONLY thing you can manage is who and what you choose to spend your time with and what you spend your time doing.

If you want to feel accomplished, productive, efficient, and successful whether at home, at work, or just in your day to day life you must first realize that your time is exactly that, your time. You can give it all away to the demands of the day, your employees, your family, your work, your thoughts, social media. The list goes on and on. Or you can choose exactly what you spend your precious time doing and who you spend it with.

Time is the most precious gift we can receive. The average person lives to be about seventy-seven years old. Remember, that's the average. Many people will never live to see seventy-seven.

Seventy-seven years equates to 4,004 weeks. That's right, 4,004 weeks. Take a moment to think about your age. How many weeks do you have left? The reality is you don't know how many weeks, days, hours, or even minutes you have left.

I walked into work Tuesday morning and sat at Patty's desk as I did every morning. She was always so bright, cheerful, energetic, loving, and a faithful servant of God. A conversation with Patty was an electrifying jump start to every day.

This morning Patty and I were sharing stories of our mothers. Both Patty and I lost our mothers at a young age. I shared with Patty how angry I was at God for a very long time for taking my mother from my father, and her three daughters at such a young age. I asked if she had ever felt the same.

Without hesitation, Patty said, "Absolutely not, God is the Author and Creator of our lives, our stories. He knows the beginning, the middle and the end. He knows how long or short our story will be."

I was in awe of Patty's faith, as I often was. Patty and I finished our conversation and I went to work like I had done every other day, not knowing that my life and Patty's was about to change forever.

8

YOUR LIFE DEPENDS ON IT

The next morning Patty wasn't at her desk. She was never late. In fact, she was always the first one to arrive. We tried to reach Patty over the next several hours, becoming more worried with each unanswered phone call. Finally, we received a call from Patty's husband. Patty had been hospitalized and was now on life support. She had been taken to the hospital the evening before (the very day we had that conversation) with flu-like symptoms which continued to get worse throughout the day. We all began to pray and continued to pray for the next several days and eventually weeks. We received updated phone calls each week and with each call, Patty's condition fluctuated. There were days with no response and there were days filled with excitement when we thought she was on the road to recovery and would soon be back to work.

Sadly, Patty was never able to return to work. She was never able to return home to her family. Within three weeks Patty went to be with the Lord, at only 2,028 weeks of age.

Again, how many weeks, days, or minutes do you have left? How will you spend them? Who will you spend them with?

Now more than ever, in today's world of high-demand, fast-pace and instant gratification you must protect and prioritize your time. Begin right now, this very minute. You're not promised another.

My brother-in-law Jeff was driving home one sunny afternoon when his truck stopped running. After being stranded for several hours Jeff decided to call a tow truck. Mike arrived within 30-minutes, loaded Jeff's truck on the trailer, invited Jeff to ride in the front of his truck with him and they were on their way. Mike was genuine and jovial. He shared his experiences as a driver, a father, and a husband as he drove Jeff home. They pulled in the driveway. Mike got out of the truck, shook Jeff's hand and thanked him for allowing him to chat with him during their travel and began to unload the truck. Jeff realized he didn't have his wallet and went inside to get his wallet so he could pay Mike. When Jeff walked back out to pay Mike it was too late. Mike had a heart attack while he was unloading Jeff's truck. In an instant, he was gone. Mike lived for 2,600 weeks.

Laura was out with her friends enjoying her teenage life. After driving through the country roads enjoying the scenery she pulled on to the highway and was hit by an RV that instantly took her life. Laura was gone after only 884 weeks.

My dear friend Lisa lived 2,236 weeks and my sweet mother was taken after only 2,444 weeks.

Every moment we are blessed to have is precious. We must choose to say yes to only those people and activities that we place value in, that allow us to fulfill our purpose, and live the life we were intended to live.

You may be thinking, *you don't understand. I have to work. Taking care of the kids, house, dinner, laundry, chores, my job (or jobs), are so demanding of my time. I couldn't ever just not do any of these things.*

I've been there. I've lived that overwhelming life. The difference is that I have come to realize that above all, time is precious, I am not promised another second, and it is me, and only me, who can choose how I spend my time by consciously choosing what and who I will say yes to.

And it is you and only you who can choose how you spend your time and what you will say yes and no to.

Are you saying yes to hours of commuting every day and no to hours or time with your family?

If you're thinking, *Crystel, I have to! I have bills to pay,* I'm going to challenge you again. You do not HAVE to. You <u>choose</u> to. You could sell or give away all your worldly possessions and live on the streets even if you have children. I'm not saying that's an ideal or even safe way to live. What I am saying is that your lifestyle is your choice.

I know hundreds of people who commute every day, spending two to four hours a day in their car, fussing about traffic, complaining about their commute and their lack of time to "get anything done". My question is always the same. Then why do you do it? Why do you choose to spend 40-80 hours every month doing something that frustrates you and takes up the time that you could be doing the things you enjoy? Their answer is always the same. Because I have bills to pay. Or because I can't make the same amount of money working close to home. Here's my answer. It is because they value their large home, or expensive vehicle, or travel, or luxury items more than they value time with their family, friends, or even relaxing. It doesn't make them right or wrong. It's just the simple truth. The sooner you come to your own truth about what you value. The easier saying yes (simultaneous no) will become.

How do you choose what and who you will say yes and simultaneous no to?

The first step is to make a list of all the people, activities, and things that you value most. If time was endless each day, who are the people you would spend your time with, what are the activities you would spend your time doing, and what are the things you are willing to trade your time to have?

Unless you've created streams of passive income (which you must if you haven't already) begin to think about each purchase you make in terms of time. If you're a salary or hourly employee, calculate what your current employer pays you each hour. If you make $50.00 an hour and want to make a $500.00 purchase, you've just traded 10 hours of your time for that investment. Is it worth it? It may be. Again, these are the things you value.

Michael complained for years that he really wanted to spend time training his horses, but he just didn't have time. This was a lie Michael continued to tell himself for years. He lived frustrated, overwhelmed, and angry every single day, complaining that he worked too much, so he didn't have enough hours in the day to work and train his horses. The reality was that he spent 5-7 hours watching television every evening. Michael had more than enough time every day to spend training his horses. He just placed a higher priority on, and valued relaxing in bed and watching television more. Michael also spent at least 15-30 minutes a day complaining that he didn't get enough sleep because he worked too late and needed time to unwind with the television before he went to bed. He also spent years saying he wanted to work out, to eat healthy, and to feel better. More lies. Michael eats fast food for breakfast, lunch, and dinner – because "he doesn't have time to cook or go to the grocery store". Michael also spent years complaining about his finances saying he never had enough money to travel and do the things he wanted in life. While he spent as much as $50.00 a day eating those meals at restaurants every day. Michael's list should have looked like this.

People I Value	Activities I Value
Me	Work
	Relaxing in bed
	Watching Television
	Convenient fast food

Michael isn't unique in his thinking. Both men and women tell themselves these lies. Again, because it's easier to blame than to take ownership of our decisions and our time. Now it's time for you to take ownership and make your list of your valuables.

People I Value	Activities I Value	Things I Value

Who and what is on your list? God? Your Spouse? Your children? Your hobbies and interests? Your bucket list? Your work? Your home? Your shoe collection? No matter what is on your list, it's your list. If you were able to be honest with yourself – this is actually what's important and valuable to <u>you</u>.

The second step is to decide how many hours you have, to spend with the people and activities on your list and reserve that time in your schedule.

Remember those 4,0004 weeks? If you sleep eight hours a night you only have 2,670 weeks while you're awake (of the 4,004 weeks) to <u>live</u> your life. Is it sinking in yet? Let me remind you that if you're commuting two hours each day, you're spending 72 weeks a year in your car. If you're spending four hours a day commuting, you're spending 149 weeks a year in your car. I'm not saying to quit your job or stop commuting. I'm saying that you must be aware of where you're spending your time and stop lying to yourself about what you find value in.

Now that you've discovered how many weeks you may have you must reserve time for each of those people, activities, or purchases.

You'll need a system to keep you accountable. Trust me. While it's easy to <u>say</u> that you're going to spend your time with your loved ones and friends, doing the things you enjoy in life or accomplishing the steps to fulfill your dreams, it can be a challenge to actually do it.

There are simple options for reserving your time. I prefer the Google calendar method. Use a calendar that works for you. Here's the key. <u>You must block your time and build your schedule *before* someone asks for your time.</u>

Open your Google calendar and start scheduling reoccurring times for who and what is valuable to you. If going to the gym every day is a valuable use of your time schedule it on your calendar at the same time every day, a time that will ensure your success.

You can't go to the gym every day? Of course, you can. The reality is you choose not to. It's a choice. You simply don't value daily time at the gym and it's not a priority in your life if you're saying you can't. That's okay. Remember, it's your time, it's your life, and only you can decide what is important to you. Just stop telling yourself the subliminal lie that you don't have time to go to the gym. And if the gym is on your list of most valuables you must remove it. Again, it's okay. Admitting that the gym, losing weight, or getting physically fit aren't priorities right now will free you of the I really need to get to the gym guilt.

Practice this exercise with everyone and everything on your list. If you aren't willing to schedule a time for it, it's just not a priority.

Now that you have your list of most valuables and you have scheduled recurring time on your calendar you must stick to it!

If today someone asked to have lunch with you how would you respond? Let me guess. Sure, what works for you? You've just given power over your time to someone else. Let the frustration and internal conversations begin! Yet we do it, over, and over again.

Have a play date for the kids? Sure, when would be good for you? Need a ride to work? Of course, when do I need to pick you up? Need to talk to someone? Call me any time. Want some help around the house? Certainly! I could use a break from cleaning mine. Take the kids to their sporting events? Sure, we can just grab fast food on the way. Work late? Oh, yes. I'm a team player! Team mom? Without even asking how much time is required. Yes! Sound familiar?

Going forward you must go directly to your schedule. If having lunch with your friends or colleagues is one of the things you placed value on it should have time reserved on your schedule. Here's your new response. Sure, I have (day) at this time or (day) at this time. Which one works best for you?

Think about the last time you made an appointment with your doctor. The office manager didn't say sure we can see you. When would you like to come? They gave you a few dates to choose from and because it was a priority, something you valued, you chose to give them your time based on their availability.

Imagine if medical practices scheduled their patients like women schedule their lives. Rather than waiting an hour to see our physician. We may be waiting hours, have missed appointments, and work with doctors and nurses who are just as frustrated and overwhelmed as we are as women with our "lack of time".

Be prepared for resistance. The person asking for your time probably doesn't think like this. They may offer you another day if your original dates aren't available for them. Stick to your schedule. Remember it's your schedule, your time, your weeks. Look at the next week on your calendar and give them two more options. Eventually, the day and time that you will offer will work, or it won't. You must decide what's the most valuable use of your time, your weeks, your hours, and your minutes.

From this very moment every time someone asks of your time before you respond ask yourself, If I say yes to this person, task, or buying this thing, what am I truly saying no to? If the answer is yes, check your schedule. Is this something that I value enough to have reserved time in my life for? If the answer is again yes put it on your schedule. Yes, you must physically reserve the time. If this is something you recently decided that you value (because our values and priorities change) you must then decide what this new value will replace AND replace it on your schedule. I've included two sample schedules on the next pages. It's up to you to create your schedule with time re-served for the people and activities that you value.

It's your time, your weeks, your days, your moments, and your seconds. You must decide, prioritize, plan, and pro-tect it as if your life depends on it. Because it absolutely does!

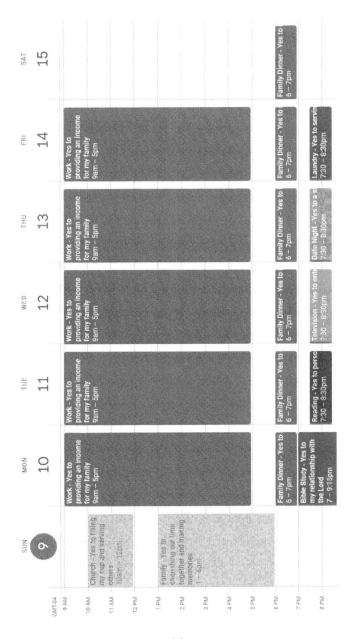

GMT-04	SUN 9	MON 10	TUE 11	WED 12	THU 13	FRI 14	SAT 15
9 AM	Prayer - Yes to the Lord 9 – 10am	Prayer - Yes to the Lord 9 – 10am	Prayer - Yes to the Lord 9 – 10am	Prayer - Yes to the Lord 9 – 10am	Prayer - Yes to the Lord 9 – 10am	Prayer - Yes to the Lord 9 – 10am	Prayer - Yes to the Lord 9 – 10am
10 AM	Church - Yes to filling my cup and serving others 10am – 12pm	Marketing - Yes to growing my business 10 – 11:30am	Reading - Yes to professional Growth 10 – 11:30am	Client meeting - Yes to serving 10 – 11:30am	Client meeting - Yes to serving 10 – 11:30am	I chose - Yes to me 10am – 3pm	
11 AM							
12 PM		Business or Friend Lunch 12 – 1pm	Business or Friend Lunch 12 – 1pm	Business or Friend Lunch 12 – 1pm	Business or Friend Lunch 12 – 1pm		
1 PM	Family - Yes to cherishing our time together and making memories – 6pm	Billing & Invoicing - Yes to getting paid for my work 1:30 – 3:15pm	Product Development - Yes to Innovation 1:30 – 3:15pm	Client meeting - Yes to serving 1:30 – 3pm	Client meeting - Yes to serving 1:30 – 3pm		
2 PM							
3 PM							
4 PM		Gym - Yes to my health 4 – 5pm	Gym - Yes to my health 4 – 5pm	Gym - Yes to my health 4 – 5pm	Gym - Yes to my health 4 – 5pm	Gym - Yes to my health 4 – 5pm	
5 PM							
6 PM		Family Dinner - Yes to 6 – 7pm	Family Dinner - Yes to 6 – 7pm	Family Dinner - Yes to 6 – 7pm	Family Dinner - Yes to 6 – 7pm	Family Dinner - Yes to 6 – 7pm	Family Dinner - Yes to 6 – 7pm
7 PM		Bible Study - Yes to my relationship with the Lord 7 – 9:15pm	Reading - Yes to personal 7:30 – 8:30pm	Television - Yes to ent 7:30 – 8:30pm	Date Night - Yes to a si 7:30 – 8:30pm	Laundry - Yes to servi 7:30 – 8:30pm	
8 PM							

9

HAVE YOU LOST YOUR MIND?

I sat in the courtroom in disbelief, overwhelmed with sadness, and filled with anxiety about what was about to happen. In the next thirty minutes, our lives would change forever. The judge would give his final ruling for our divorce and child custody.

After what seemed like an eternity I heard the words that immediately lifted the 1,000-pound weight off of my shoulders, the worry that had consumed my thoughts, taken hours of my sleep and inches from my waist over the last several months, "Primary physical custody is granted to Mrs. Combs." I collapsed in my chair with an audible sigh of relief.

I didn't hear much after that <u>until,</u> "No, Mrs. Combs, you may not continue to operate a daycare from your home as your primary source of income."

I was a stay at home mother and operated a daycare for thirteen years from my home and loved every second of it. I was inspected by and registered with the state. I reported my income every year through our joint tax return. Yet the judge said that there was too much opportunity in my home-based business to hide income from Mr. Combs. He ordered that I get a J.O.B.

How could I get a job? How could I leave my children? Hadn't they been through enough? For thirteen years I was the mother who woke them up every morning, made them breakfast, put them on the bus, welcomed them home after school, sat with them to do their homework, tucked them in every night, went on every field trip, volunteered at their school, took them to every sporting event, extracurricular activity, never missed a baseball or football game, wrestling match, concert, track meet, talent show, spent countless summer days playing, going to the pool, the park, the drive-in, the library, spent sleepless nights caring for them while they were sick, encouraging them when they challenged. And now I would have to give my time to a company? They would dictate what I could spend time with my children?

It was the judge's order. And I was willing to do whatever it took to follow those orders and ensure that my children were provided for in a way the court deemed necessary.

I picked up a newspaper on the way home, (that's how we found jobs in the early '90s), locked myself in my bedroom, and buried myself in the classifieds for the next hour.

> **Wanted**: *Forklift Operator, Second Shift,*
> *Tuesday through Saturday.*

> **Opening**: *Bindery Operator Assistant,*
> *Third Shift Sunday through Thursday.*

> **Hiring**: *Cashier/Clerk, Varying Schedule,*
> *Must be willing to work evenings and weekends.*

The more I read the more discouraged I became. I knew I had to have a job that provided "reportable income" as the judge had stated. I also knew that I would never work those hours and leave my children in daycare for someone else to care for.

Then I saw it!

> **Wanted**: *Teller Wachovia Bank, Part-Time*
> *Monday - Friday, some Saturdays required.*

This was the perfect job! In the '90s banks were open from 9:00 a.m. until 2:00 p.m. I could wake my children up, share breakfast with them, put them on the bus, be home in time to get them off the bus and spend every evening just like we always did! And my children would spend every other weekend with their father. I was certain the bank would let me work every other Saturday. This was an answer to my prayers.

I ran to my car, drove to the bank, and filled out an application. Within a week I received a call from Mary, the branch manager from Wachovia Bank, to schedule an interview. I remember thinking wow, that was easy!

I walked in Friday morning confident that I was about to land the job! After all, my in-home daycare had given me experience in budgeting, scheduling, balancing a checkbook (Yes, we did that in the 90's too,) and customer service. I was certainly the person for the job. After the interview, Mary said, "Let me give you a quick tour of our office and introduce you to your new coworkers, that is as long as your background and credit check come back okay." I was elated! We took a quick tour. I met a few very pleasant women and ran home to call my friend to share my great news!

Three days later the phone rang. The caller ID said Wachovia Bank. I could hardly contain my excitement! It was Mary! She was calling to give me my schedule! I gathered myself, answered the phone in my most pleasant customer service voice.

"Hello, this is Crystel."

"Hi Crystel, this is Mary. How are you today?"

"I'm wonderful Mary. Thank you for asking. How are you?"

"I'm good, Crystel. However, I'm calling to tell you that at this time you are not the right fit for our bank."

All I could muster out was, "*What?*"

Mary repeated herself, "You're not the right fit for the bank."

"Not the right fit?" I asked. "I'm confused. You showed me my new teller station. You introduced me to my new coworkers. You said you were highly impressed with me. Why am I not the right fit for your bank three days later?"

"Crystel, you have a medical bill in collections on your credit report and unfortunately, that makes you a high risk in the banking industry."

"High risk? I don't understand."

"It puts the bank at risk for embezzlement," she explained.

"Embezzlement? Do you think I would steal? What on earth makes you think that?"

Mary replied, "You may seize an opportunity to take from the cash your responsible for at the bank to pay your debt."

I don't know where it came from but the next words out of my mouth were, "Are you crazy? Seriously, have you lost your mind? First of all, I didn't even know that I had a medical bill in collections. I just refinanced my home and had impeccable credit. Second, I can fix this. Please let me fix this. I will call and pay the medical bill today."

"I'm sorry, Crystel. There's nothing I can do. I hope you have a good day."

And that was that. I asked Mary for a job and got a big fat no.

10

THIRTY-SEVEN DOLLARS

I hung up the phone in disbelief. How could she tell me no? No to the job. No to providing an income to support my children. No to fixing the problem.

I knew that banking was a job that would allow me to earn an income, provide for my children, AND still be home to care for them. I also knew that if this bank thought I would steal from them there was a good chance that every other bank would think so too.

I don't even remember how now but I got a copy of my credit report. (CreditKarma.com didn't exist in the '90s.) I can remember opening the envelope, unfolding the report and sure enough, there it was, the medical bill, in collections for $37.00.

My first response was anger. How could the hospital ruin my chances of getting a job and providing for my children over $37.00? How could the bank say no over $37.00? That frustration lasted for about five minutes.

I quickly realized that it wasn't the hospital's responsibility to pay my debts. It wasn't the bank's fault that I had overlooked it. Both the responsibility and the fault were mine.

I called the 800 number on the credit report, got the address, wrote a check, and drove to the post office. I was not going to get a no from another bank.

Forty-six days later I received a letter of satisfaction and felt confident to once again begin applying for jobs.

> **Wanted**: *Part-Time Teller, First Virginia Bank.*
> *Apply Within*

And apply within I did!

I immediately explained to Brenda, the branch manager, that I may still have a $37.00 collection on my credit report.

Oh, honey, we've all had challenges with our health that lead to things like that. I don't think that's going to be a problem.

Once again three days later the phone rang with the caller ID, First Virginia Bank.

"Hi, Crystel. This is Brenda. How are you?"

"Hi, Brenda. I'm well. Thank you. How are you?"

"I'm great because I'm excited to welcome you to our team!"

"Oh, thank you! Thank you, Brenda! I'm excited too! When can I start?"

"I'll see you on Monday morning at 9:00!"

I did it! I got a job that will provide for my children and allow me to spend every moment they're not in school with them. Well, except in the summer and I'll figure that out soon enough.

Our immediate <u>reaction</u> to hearing the word no is usually either to tell ourselves a lie now, *I'm never going to be able to get a bank job!* or to blame others How could they ruin my chance of getting this job?

In order to understand the power of no you must under-stand that <u>you have the power</u>. You have the power to <u>choose</u> your feeling, your response, your opportunity, and your outcome.

I grew personally and professionally over the next seven years of my career at that bank. I became one of the top producers, climbed the corporate ladder, was about to climb another rung and advance to branch manager until again, I was told no.

My existing Manager, Vic, walked into the office around 10:30 that morning as he had done every day for the last seven years. Except for this time, instead of the usual "Good morning," he said, "I can't do this anymore. I'm leaving." And just like that, he turned around, walked back out and I never saw Vic again. Within a few hours, we received notice that Vic had quit. While I wasn't surprised that Vic had decided to leave the bank, what happened next was a huge surprise.

Robin, the existing area manager walked in, stormed over to me, bent over my desk, getting as close to my face as she could without touching nose to nose and said, "Vic is gone. I'm your new boss now and I just fired your best friend Debbie. Here's what I expect. I expect that you'll run both offices just like you have been. I expect that if the doors are open you will be here working. Oh, and the Virginia Labor Laws don't require that I give breaks. So, keep some snacks in your drawer in case you get hungry." Then she turned around and walked out.

I sat there for a few minutes in disbelief and immediately decided that I needed to apply for Vic's job as branch manager. If this is the person they were going to put in place as our leader, I had to fill that need as soon as possible.

I waited and watched daily for the opening – except there wouldn't be an official opening until a year later as they occasionally sent other branch managers to fill Vic's position. This left me to manage, schedule, support, and lead two offices for the next year. Then in October of the next year there it was! The branch manager job posting. I immediately applied.

I was confident in my abilities and application. If I'm being honest, I thought I was a shoo-in. I had been there for seven years. It had been a year since Vic had left and I was, in fact, running both offices. I increased loan production 700% and deposit production 300%. Every employee from both offices wrote their own letter of recommendation. Yep, I was the one for the job!

I walked into the second office the next Monday morning and immediately knew something was up. Every one of the tellers looked up at me when I walked in the door like they were being held hostage.

"Hey everyone! How are all my amazing friends today?"

Almost simultaneously, without saying a word, they all cut their eyes to the left toward my office. I looked over at my office (which had glass walls) and noticed a man walking around the office who appeared to be talking to himself.

"Who's that?"

Mary finally squeaked out, "Um, our new branch manager."

"What?"

"Yes, Crystel, he's from North Carolina. He's been walking around with that earpiece in his ear and talking on his cell phone all day. He shushes us when we try to talk to him. We can't even get approvals because he won't get off the phone. It's terrible. And we're so sorry you didn't get the job."

"I… what… didn't get the job?"

"You didn't know? Oh my gosh. I'm so sorry. I thought they would have told you before they sent a new manager."

60

"It's okay. Let me see what's going on. Maybe he's just the branch manager of this office and they're going to make me the branch manager of the other office. After all, there are two offices and I've been managing them both. Having two managers would be a wonderful thing!"

I walked into his office and extended my hand only to confirm what the others had said. He swiped his hand mid-air a few times, waving me back out the door as he continued to walk and talk on his phone.

I was dumbfounded. I couldn't even fathom treating another human being like that. I did as his wave commanded and left his office, and then walked straight to the phone and called our area director, Wilborn.

I was sure that Wilborn would have a good explanation of why this man seemed to be so dismissive of others and why I hadn't received the news that they had hired him to manage the first office and share the news that I would manage the other office.

I shouldn't have been so sure.

"Hey, Wilborn. How are you?" was my greeting.

"I'm good, Crystel. How are you?"

"I'm a little confused and was hoping you could shed some light for me."

"Sure. What can I help you with?" he replied.

"I believe I just met the new branch manager at the Fairfax Pike office, Mike."

"Oh, Mike! Yes, he's great. His numbers are phenomenal. You're going to learn a lot working for him."

"Learn a lot working for him?"

"Yes, Mike is your new branch manager."

"My new branch manager? I thought you may have hired him to manage Fairfax Pike and were going to promote me to branch manager of Main Street."

(Here it comes.)

"No, Crystel. We've hired Mike to manage both branches."

"So, I'm not getting promoted to branch manager even though I have a letter of recommendation from every employee at both offices and my numbers are off the charts AND I have been managing both offices for a year?"

(Here it comes again.)

"No."

"That's it? Just no?" I remarked.

"Well, what else can I say, Crystel? He's just the better choice for the job."

And that was that.

I hung up the phone and noticed that again all of my colleagues were looking at me with concern.

"What are you going to do?" I asked myself.

I'm going to pray about it. I'm going to get excited about finding another opportunity with a bank that appreciates my talent and efforts. Just like I did seven years ago.

I left that day and began to pray and praise God for what He had in store for me. I chose joy and lots of it!

I got home that evening and began to search the newspapers once again.

> Wanted: Assistant Branch Manager
> Marathon Bank

I didn't even read the rest.

On my lunch break the next day (because now I could take a lunch break since we had another manager at the Fairfax Pike office) I drove to Marathon Bank and applied for the assistant branch manager position.

Again, I waited. And again, I received a phone call. This time it was from an amazing woman named Leah Day and she wanted to meet with me for an interview!

A week later I was sitting with Leah, confident in my abilities, excited about the opportunity, and nervous about the outcome. After all, I had been confident about all of those things before and received a no.

This time was different. Leah called and asked that I meet with her again. I thought they wanted a second interview. This was great! Progress!

I walked into Leah's office the next afternoon and she explained that she didn't think I was the best fit for the assistant branch manager role.

Before I had an opportunity to respond or even digest what I had just heard she said, "You are so very talented. We know there is something special about you and would like to create a new role just for you. It's a Traveling Manager."

"A Traveling Manager? What is that?" I asked.

"We need someone like you to be a leader when our other branch managers are out or need support," she replied.

"Other branch managers? This is a branch manager position?"

"Yes, you would have the title of branch manager and you would be the manager at each branch based on which manager was on vacation, out for leave, or in need of additional management."

"So, let me get this straight. I wouldn't be an assistant manager? I would be a branch manager?"

"Yes, how does that sound to you?"

"It sounds perfect! It's more than I had hoped for!"

"Okay, now let's talk salary," Leah continued.

"Oh yes! I hadn't even thought about that!"

The salary was $10,000.00 more a year than I would have made as a branch manager if I had stayed with the other bank!

It took me ten minutes to drive back to the office and two minutes to type and send my resignation letter – which I did with gratitude. I thanked my current employer for be-lieving enough in me to give me my first teller job. I thanked them for the education and experience they gave me for seven years. And I thanked them for the oppor-tunity to develop my talent, by telling me no, at another financial institution.

Had I chosen to feel angry and resentful the outcome would have been nothing less than another seven years working for the man who cared more his career than his employees. The choice was mine. And the choice is yours. How will you choose to feel when you hear your next no?

11

CHANGE THAT ATTITUDE MISSY

How do you feel when you're told no?

- Frustrated?
- Angry?
- Resentful?
- Not valuable?
- Sad?
- Rejected?
- All of the above?

Remember, you must be honest with yourself. No more subliminal lies. No more blaming. If you want the power of no. You must stop giving your power to the detrimental feeling choices you've been making.

Yes, I said the feeling <u>choices</u> that you've been making.

Tammy introduced me to her friend Joy and asked me to share the conversation she and I were having in the moments before Joy arrived.

I was happy to!

"Tammy and I were just discussing how our feelings are our choice. We can choose to be angry or happy. We can choose to feel frustrated or grateful."

Joy's response was typical, "You can't help how you feel. They're your feelings. You can't control them."

"It isn't about control," I answered, "It is about making a choice. The two are very different."

"It isn't a choice! They're your feelings. You can't choose them either."

"Sure, you can. May I ask you a couple of questions?"

With a sigh, "Yes."

"How would you feel if your husband slapped you in the face?"

"Angry!"

"Great. How would you feel if a 6-month-old baby slapped you in the face?"

"Well, nothing, it's a baby."

"Exactly. In both scenarios, you were slapped in the face. The only difference was how you chose to feel."

"That's different."

"How is it different?"

"Well, the baby probably did it by accident."

"You're telling me that how you feel is based on the intention of others?"

"Well, yes."

I continued, "So they are actually the ones who have the power to choose how you feel?"

"Well, no."

"Right. You are the only one who has the power to choose your feelings."

"I still don't agree." Joy stated.

At that moment we were both called back for our pedicures. I hope to finish this conversation with Joy if we meet again.

The truth, and it will set you free, is that you have the opportunity to choose whether you feel anger or whether you feel joy, curiosity, empathy, or any other emotion.

As women, we often replace the word, feeling, with attitude. Especially when it comes to our children, spouses, friends, and coworkers.

The *English-Language Learners* definition of attitude is "the way you think and <u>feel</u> about someone or something. : <u>a feeling</u> or way of thinking that affects a person's behavior."

While the two words are interchangeable, using the word attitude frees us, tells us a lie, that attitudes are our choice and feelings are not.

You better change that attitude missy! I think I've been told that more times than I've have the privilege of waking up (especially during my teen years).

My best friend, Lisa Marler, had just turned sixteen. She called me to share her exciting news. She had just registered to take Driver's Ed. Behind the Wheel, a class in Virginia, that would allow her to get her driver's license. My excitement grew when she said that I should take the class with her! What a marvelous idea! After all, we were best friends and should achieve this accomplishment together!

I hung up the phone and ran to the kitchen to share this great opportunity with my mother. "Mom! I'm going to take Driver's Ed with Lisa! It's only $350.00 and then I'll be ready to drive!"

My mother looked at me like a dog that was hearing a high-pitched noise that only the dog could hear, head cockeyed, eyebrows raised and said, "Driver's Ed?"

"C'mon. You have to know what Driver's Ed is!"

"I do know what it is. But you can't take Driver's Ed."

"I can't take Driver's Ed?" I asked. "Why not?!"

"Because you're only thirteen years old," Mom told me.

"Yes, I'm thirteen and if I take it now, I'll be ready to drive before I'm sixteen!"

"I think you're missing the point. You're not legally allowed to drive until your sixteen. This class is a driving class. So, you legally can't take the class."

This was the dumbest thing I had ever heard from my mother's lips. Why was she being so mean? Why was she keeping me from this achievement? Why couldn't she see that Lisa and I were a team and we had to do this together? Why did she insist on telling me no?"

I continued to argue with her for the next hour or so until I finally realized that she was not going to give. I stomped back to my room, slammed the door (so she would know just how mad she had made me) and called Lisa with the sad, sad, news.

I then proceeded back to the living room to tell my mother exactly how disappointed and angry I was at her for taking this incredible opportunity from me.

"You better change your attitude missy."

I can remember thinking, *change my attitude? You're the one who's telling me no! You're the one who's making me mad!* The reality was that I was the one who <u>chose</u> my attitude. I chose my feelings. At that moment I decided that whatever my mother said, didn't say, did, or didn't do, the no, was more important than my happiness and my wellbeing.

Anger has been related to cardiovascular disease, Atherosclerosis, and high blood pressure. The next time someone tells you no and "makes you angry", I challenge you to look at yourself and ask why you are choosing this attitude, this anger, this feeling over your own joy and health.

Your attitude, your feelings are yours and yours alone. No one can "make you mad".

Don't believe me? Think about that person you know who always seems to be so happy. You know that person, the one whose glass is always half full, that friend or colleague who everyone refers to as the one with the bubbly personality.

Some may say, "They were just born like that." Maybe they were. Or maybe they chose an attitude of joy, gratitude, and resolution in every circumstance. Maybe while they are standing in the only open, and long line, at the grocery store, they chose to see it as an opportunity to interact on social media and chat with friends or even make new acquaintances while waiting in line. Maybe when someone says harsh words to them, they chose to be curious about that person and wonder why they feel the need to say such things. Maybe they chose to understand why the person is so upset and see the opportunity to improve their own actions – to better the relationship. Maybe when they are told no, they choose to feel curious about how they can accomplish what they want.

Legend has it that Colonel Sanders received 1,009 no's before he finally received a yes. Do you think he would have continued to pursue his dreams after the first, second, or even third no – by feeling angry or frustrated? I'm sure that with each no he felt more determined, ambitious, and excited about the next opportunity to present his recipe.

We're told no in various forms. We must recognize that in many circumstances where we choose to become angry, frustrated, defeated, it's a result of someone telling us no, even if they didn't directly say no.

Michael Jordan wasn't allowed to play varsity basketball early on. He didn't choose to blame the basketball coach. He didn't choose to blame his height, as the coaches did. He did choose to feel sad that afternoon. However, he did immediately choose to feel determined and ultimately went on to be one of the world's most successful basketball stars of all time.

Steve Jobs was fired from Apple, the company he had created. (No, we don't want you to work here any longer.) Steve has been quoted to say, "I didn't see it then, but it turned out that getting fired from Apple was the best thing that could have ever happened to me. The heaviness of being successful was replaced by the lightness of being a beginner again, less sure about everything. It freed me to enter one of the most creative periods of my life."

Walt Disney was fired from the Kansas City Star in 1919 because his editor said he "lacked imagination and had no good ideas." (No, your ideas aren't good enough.) The world as we know it would be a very different place if Walt had decided to choose sadness or anger and give up on his dream. We wouldn't have Disney World, Disney Land, The Disney Experience training, Mickey Mouse, Beauty and the Beast, Cinderella, Snow White, or the other 146 Disney movies that have inspired us all over the last eight decades.

My soon to be ex-husband (yes, there will be another divorce) said no to our lifelong commitment of marriage with his abuse and affairs. I could choose to feel sad, broken, resentful and defeated. And trust me for some time that is exactly what I chose to feel. I'm not saying it's easy. I'm saying choosing your feelings will directly impact your life.

Today I choose to feel grateful. Grateful for the opportunity to gain a new daughter through that marriage. Grateful to have had the experience of living on a farm. Grateful to now have the opportunity to live in peace. I choose joy – the joy of waking up each day with the sound of grandbabies running through the house rather than the wrath of my spouse. The joy of having so many loving and supportive friends. I choose happiness – the happiness that comes from within – a happiness that is not reliant on the approval of my spouse. I choose love – love that is unconditional, that even today prays for the man that tried to destroy me, my family, and even his own daughter.

The choice is yours. You may choose to feel sadness, anger, frustration. You may choose to feel defeated. You may choose to give the power of no to someone or something else. Or you may choose to be curious about the opportunity, to feel joy, happiness, and gratefulness about the all that you already are, have and will be.

So how do you choose your feelings?

12

I AM GOING STRAIGHT TO HELL

My daughter of another mother, Alyssa, is a vibrant, intelligent, fun-loving, young woman, who has brought great joy to our family. I love Alyssa as if I had given birth to her myself. While the legal term for our relationship is stepmother and stepdaughter, we define our relationship as mother and daughter. There is no step. We have a strong bond and an incredible relationship. We love to spend time just hanging out, catching up, sharing our challenges, successes, and laughing uncontrollably.

Alyssa visits her father and I a few times a year. And each time, Alyssa lives as many traveling teenagers do, from her suitcase, even though she has her own room with more than enough room and storage for her clothes and any other belongings she decides to bring each visit.

I was working from home that hot summer day. It was ninety degrees outside. And living in a farmhouse with no central air forced me to take a break, refill my water and get up to enjoy a few minutes of the outdoors, which was cooler than the office I worked from.

As I was walking by Alyssa's room, her bedroom door was open just enough to frame the mounds of clothes, piles of makeup, unmade bed, open food containers, and a trail of Cheez-Its. I pushed the door open just a tad more only to be hit in the face with the stench of a rabbit cage that was fuming in the sweltering heat and smelled like it hadn't been changed in weeks.

My initial reaction (choice of feelings) was anger and frustration. I had cleaned her room, put fresh linens on the bed, and even decorated her room only a week ago, in excitement for her arrival.

How could she do this to her room? How could she dismiss everything that I had done to show her how much I loved her?

I sat on her unmade bed, feeling unappreciated and unloved as I scanned the mess over and over again. The internal conversation began. *Gosh, I love her so much. Why would she do this to me? She knows I'm busy. She knows I don't have time to clean up after her. She's only here for a few weeks. How hard is it to pick up after yourself? Especially if it's only for a couple of weeks.*

And then my next profound, painful, and life-changing moment happened. It was like I heard God say, "Wake up! You are so right! She IS here. You will only have her with you for a few weeks. You do love her."

It was at that moment that I realized that a clean bedroom didn't change the fact that I loved her with all my heart. It didn't mean that she didn't love me. And it certainly didn't mean the world would come to an end.

What it DID mean was that I was incredibly blessed! I had a wonderful daughter who chose to spend her summer with us! This beautiful teenager, who could have spent her summer with friends and having the time of her life CHOSE to spend it with me and her father! And I had a career that allowed me to work from home, that gave me the opportunity to clean her room! I broke down in tears, overwhelmed with gratitude. I must have sat on that un-made bed, literally on a heap of twisted and piled sheets, pillows, and blankets for fifteen minutes in awe of how blessed and grateful I was for this opportunity!

Yes, opportunity! I bounced off the bed with excitement and began to clean Alyssa's room. I tore everything off of her bed, washed, dried and made her bed as if I was making the bed for a princess' arrival. I moved her furniture (and she has some hefty furniture) cleaned the trash and dust from underneath, swept and mopped until the floors shined. I dusted every dustable piece of furniture and baseboard. (Yes, I know I just made up the word dustable.) I cleared the feces and shavings from the rabbit cage, sprayed it down with the water hose until it shined like grandma's silverware. Her room was prepared for a princess, our princess.

Within minutes the internal conversations started again. You know the devil likes to get you talking to yourself often. *What if Alyssa is upset that I cleaned her room? What if she feels like I invaded her privacy?* Teenagers do that, ya know. *What if she thinks me cleaning her room means that she isn't capable of cleaning her room to our standards?*

Before I knew it I was walking back to my office to get a pen and paper.

"Just because I love you. Love, Mom."

I placed the note on the center of her bed. It was still missing something. Ahhh, flowers. I walked outside, cut some of the most beautiful flowers from our yard, placed them my favorite vase and set them in the center of Alyssa's dresser so that they were the first thing she saw when she walked into the room.

I felt amazing! I was filled with gratitude to have the opportunity to clean Alyssa's room. Cleaning her room meant that she chose to spend her summer with us. It meant that she was out enjoying her time. It meant that I had been blessed with an amazing career that allowed me to serve my family. I sat, this time on her perfectly made bed and thanked the Lord for Alyssa, for bringing her into my life, for the opportunity to see how blessed I was to have a messy teenage room in my home again.

I was full of gratitude and energy at this point. I wanted to do more, to serve more, to show my family how grateful I was for them. I cleaned the entire house with as much love and care as I cleaned Alyssa's room. I made their favorite dinner and placed it in the oven so it would be warm when they arrived home. I even cut more flowers and made a centerpiece and placed two candles on the table for our family dinner.

It was time to get back to work and with energy and motivation like I hadn't had in months. I must have worked for three hours before I heard Alyssa walk in the door. The next thing I heard was a loud long squeal of, "Awwwwww! You cleaned my room!" Then, bam! I felt an attack from behind. The force toppled me to the ground. It was Alyssa jumping on my back and hugging me as she yelled, "Thank you! Thank you! I love you too mom!"

That day I chose, and every day since I choose to be grateful in every circumstance.

How do I, and how can you, choose gratitude and joy over anger and frustration?

First, you MUST intentionally seek out all of the blessings in the situation. If you seek you will find. When you find yourself in a situation when someone, in their way, has told you no, grab a pen and paper. Write down all of the things that you do have the ability to do or have at that moment.

In my moment, I had Alyssa in our home. I had the opportunity to serve her. I had the opportunity to show her how to love, to feel loved. I had hands that could pick up the trash and scrub the floors, I had a career that allowed me to adjust my schedule and work from home – and I was grateful for all those things!

Next, you must choose to FOCUS on the blessings. I chose to focus on the fact that a messy teenage room meant that Alyssa was here with us. It meant that she loved us enough to want to spend time with us. It meant that we had a room that we could provide to her. (Some children don't have the luxury of having their own room.) It meant that she was out enjoying her summer. Which is exactly what we want for our children, right? We love them. We want them to enjoy their lives. Yes, we want to teach them responsibility too. We can do both, by choosing our feelings first.

Since that day I've never had to ask Alyssa to clean her room. Don't get me wrong. It isn't always princess clean. However, what is more important to us, most valuable to us, is that we do always love and are always grateful for each other.

This could have ended very differently. I could have chosen to be angry and frustrated, (yes, it's a choice) to call Alyssa and tell her how unhappy I was with her room, to make her come home and clean it. Trust me. I've done that with Alyssa before as well as with my other children.

And the result is always the same, anger, hurt, and things, lots of things, shoved under the bed at best. C'mon you just agreed with me, didn't you?

If we have the choice, why would choose anything but joy? The answer is another harsh reality. I never said the power of no is easy to obtain. I did say that it would change your life.

We choose to feel angry or frustrated or overwhelmed because it is easier to lie to ourselves and say our feelings aren't a choice. We can blame the feeling. *Oh, that girl! She's a mess! She doesn't care how hard I worked to make her room nice. She just makes me so mad!* We may get some empathy from all the time we invest in complaining to others. We may feel validated through some of those conversations. However, we will also make zero progress on the outcome that we truly want, and continue to live a life of frustration, defeat, overwhelming days and sleepless nights.

Finally, you MUST be clear that the no really was intended the way you perceived it. Alyssa's messy room wasn't how I initially perceived it. It was simply that she placed more value on spending time with her friends and family in the short amount of time that she had here each summer than she did on a clean bedroom. It had absolutely nothing to do with me.

Perception can be a joy killer! You must clarify that your perception of the situation is accurate.

My daughter, Stephanie, was in severe pain and we were instructed to immediately go to the hospital if she experienced any pain. Let me tell you Stephanie's tolerance for pain is like I've seen in no other. So, when she said we needed to go to the hospital because she was excruciating pain, I knew it was serious. We grabbed our things and made our way ever so slowly to the hospital. The pain was in Stephanie's back and legs and she struggled even to walk. We finally made it to the hospital, entered the elevator, and as the door opened, I noticed that the nurse who was on the elevator behind Stephanie was anxious to get off the elevator. She was fidgeting, huffing, and even rolling her eyes at Stephanie. I thought she doesn't even know that's my daughter. And my daughter is in extreme pain and doing the best she can. And I can see her! I went into momma bear mode. C'mon you know exactly what I'm talking about.

I looked at the fidgety, huffing and puffing eye-rolling nurse and said She's in a lot of pain. She's moving as fast as she can. There's no need for you to act like that. She looked at me for a brief moment and then proceeded to walk down the hall, still huffing and fidgeting. I couldn't believe it. How could a nurse be so unkind and uncaring?

I had to refocus my attention on Stephanie. We entered the waiting room and within minutes a nurse called, "Stephanie Combs?" I looked up to see Miss Fidgety herself calling my daughter. I thought, "Oh, no. Please, not the uncaring gruff nurse!" Stephanie walked through the waiting room with that nurse and I spent a long thirty minutes waiting for the news on how they would relieve her pain and hear how Miss Fussy-butt treated her.

Finally, Stephanie walked out. She had the smirk on her face and was shaking her head back and forth at me. My first thought was, whew, at least they've given her some relief from her pain. She seems to be feeling better. My second was, why is she looking at me like that?

By the time we met the words were already coming out of her mouth. I could hardly understand her because she was laughing so hard her words came out in broken syllables.

"You...are...go...ing...straight...to...Hell!"

What?

Again, she uttered the words through her what was at this point belly laughter, "You...are...going...straight...to Hell."

"What on earth are you talking about?"

Still laughing, "That nurse...the one you chastised in the elevator...for...for...huffing and rolling her eyes at me..."

"Yes? What about her?"

"She's an amazing nurse mom!"

"Okay, great. And that is so funny because? And I'm going to hell because?"

"Because that's who she is!"

"What? Who she is?"

"Yes, I'm not sure what it is exactly but she can't control her eye movement or breathing or fidgeting. And YOU chastised her for it! You're going straight to Hell!"

"Oh, my goodness. I AM going straight to Hell! I need to apologize to her!"

"Yes, mom. Yes, you do! And Jesus too!"

While this may be an extreme example of how our perception, right or wrong, can be a joy killer. Your perception, if you choose to allow it, can and will steal your joy minute by minute in everyday ordinary conversations, circumstances, situations, and relationships.

Michael and I were going to a social gathering for a local networking group that I belonged to.

Just as we were getting ready to walk out the door he said, "Honey, do you like this shirt?" (I've always said be careful what you ask me. You may not like my answer.)

I said, "Actually, I don't. I like the blue one better. That night turned out to be a disastrous night during our marriage."

"You don't like my shirt?"

"No, I like the blue one."

"So, you think I'm not attractive? Do you think you're a better dresser than me? Oh, Crystel is so perfect. She's going to be the best-dressed thang out there!"

"What? I...No...I don't think I'm a better dresser. I think you're incredibly handsome. What just happened?"

I'll tell you what happened. Michael's perception was that by saying I didn't like his shirt choice I was actually implying all those other horrible things, which couldn't have been further from the truth. I just didn't like the shirt.

The next time you hear the dreaded no. Check yourself and your perception. Share your perception with the person you're receiving the no from and clarify! Remember, perception can and will kill your joy!

Here's a template for the next time you're told no. Whether it's directly or indirectly. Write down what you see as the no. Initially, Alyssa's messy room said to me, *no I don't care if Mom worked hard to make sure I had a nice warm and inviting room to come home to.*

Then write down all of the blessings you already have. My blessings were all those things I shared earlier.

You will immediately see those feelings of defeat, anger, and frustration fall away and be replaced with gratitude and joy.

Next, write down what their no meant to you and clarify with the person who said no. Was that their intention? If it was, you still have the opportunity to focus on the blessing in the situation and choose to be full of joy.

Even if the nurse's intentions were to become frustrated with my daughter. I didn't have to choose to become angry. Choosing anger took attention away from my daughter. It made me sick to my stomach. And encouraged me to ultimately choose fear and more anger while I waited for Stephanie to return.

Again, how you choose to feel when you hear or <u>think</u> you hear, the word no is something that only you can do. This template will give you the opportunity to choose gratitude, joy, or any emotion that you choose over the detrimental feelings you've been choosing to blame and give your power to.

The No	My Percep-tion	The Truth	The Blessings	The Feeling I Choose

13

TODAY IS THE DAY

My dear amazing, do it all, women friends,

TODAY is the day, the pivotal and profound moment in your life when you have obtained the power of no.

Today is the day that when you are asked to be, feel, or do you will intentionally and purposefully decide and declare what saying yes means saying no to.

You will be honest with yourself and others about who and what you value most in your life.

You will take ownership and responsibility for your decisions.

You understand that you are not promised another day.

You will spend today and every day doing exactly what you truly want to be doing, with those you choose to spend your oh-so-precious time with.

You will choose joy, gratitude, and peace over frustration, anger, and guilt.

You will live the life God intended you to live, tell the story that you were created to tell, in the time that you are blessed to receive.

You have the power of no!

I want to leave you with one last power of no tool.

On the following page, you will find your power of no statement. Rip it out. Make copies. Take a picture and save it to your phone and read it daily, or even hourly, to remind yourself of your power.

— With unconditional gratitude, Crystel

Today is the day that when I am asked to be, feel, or do, I will intentionally and purposefully decide and declare what saying yes to means I will be saying no to.

I will be honest with myself and others about who and what I value most in my life.

I will take ownership and responsibility for my decisions.

I understand that I am not promised another day.

I will spend today, and every day, doing exactly what I truly want to be doing – with those I choose to spend my precious time with.

I will choose joy, gratitude, curiosity, and peace over frustration, anger, and guilt.

I will live the life God intended for me to live, tell the story that I was meant to tell, in the time that I'm blessed to receive.

I have the power of no!

ABOUT THE AUTHOR

Crystel Lynn Smith

Crystel Lynn Smith, mother of three, grandmother of four, best-selling author, inspirational speaker, high-performance business coach, and activator was born in a small town in Maryland.

At the age of six, her family moved to Middletown, Virginia, where she was raised and enjoyed the sense of family and community that her small town offered.

Crystel continues to live with her children, Brian (Bubby), Stephanie (Luvy), and grandchildren Mason (Mase), Addison (Addy Pie), Ettalynn (Etta Betta), Julius (JuJu Bean), in Virginia's beautiful Shenandoah Valley.

Crystel is driven to catapult others to achieve more than they've ever imagined and to uplift, inspire, motivate, and activate their dreams!

She has been blessed in her 20-year career with the opportunity to train (lead, motivate, inspire, and propel) over 4,000 people with an extensive track record of success.

While working with hundreds of businesses throughout her career, Crystel became an expert in analyzing business operations, finances, systems, and team (people) challenges and successes. Her expertise, coupled with her ability to inspire, prompted one of the world's largest coaching firms to recruit Crystel as a Business Coach in 2013.

In 2015, Crystel ventured into the world of writing and speaking – launching her career and passion and the dreams of others to unimaginable heights.

Crystel's devotion to revealing and sharing the truth drives her to continue to publish educational and inspirational material as well as travel across the nation, to ignite and fuel the fire that lies within us all!

Made in the USA
Monee, IL
09 May 2022

96128774R10059